D1778073

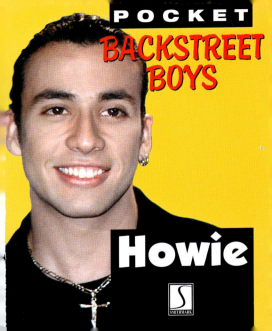

POCKET

BACKSTREET BOYS

Howie

SMITHMARK

First published in 1998 by Boxtree, an imprint of Macmillan Publishers Ltd, 25 Eccleston Place, London, SW1W 9NF and Basingstoke

Associated companies throughout the world

ISBN 0-7651-0955-7

Copyright © 1998 Boxtree

Photographs: All Action – 19, 25, 29, 37, 48, back jacket, front endpaper. Capital – 9, 32, 38. Famous – 1, 3, 5, 6, 30, 34, 41, front jacket. Redferns – 11, 12, 15, 16, 21, 22, 26, 43, 44, 47, back endpaper.

All rights reserved. No part of this publication may be reproduced, stored in or introduced into a retrieval system, or transmitted, in any form, or by any means (electronic, mechanical, photocopying, recording or otherwise) without the prior written permission of the publisher. Any person who does any unauthorized act in relation to this publication may be liable to criminal prosecution and civil claims for damage.

This edition published in 1998 by SMITHMARK Publishers, a division of U.S. Media Holdings, Inc., 115 West 18th Street, New York, NY 10011.

SMITHMARK books are available for bulk purchase for sales promotion and premium use. For details write or call the manager of special sales, SMITHMARK Publishers, 115 West 18th Street, New York, NY 10011.

9 8 7 6 5 4 3 2

Designed by Blackjacks

Printed in Hong Kong

This book is sold subject to the condition that it shall not, by way of trade or otherwise, be lent, re-sold, hired out, or otherwise circulated without the publisher's prior consent in any form of binding or cover other than that in which it is published and without a similar condition including this condition being imposed on the subsequent purchaser.

Neither the members of Backstreet Boys nor any of their representatives have had any involvement with this book

Howard
Dwaine Dorough
was born in
Orlando on
22 August 1973

Nick reckons that if he was a dog, Howie would be a chihuahua 'cos he's sweet and yappy!

The band call Howie 'Sweet D' 'cos he never says no to the fans

He has a Pekinese dog called Oscar and a cat named Christopher

Howie used to practise his hip-hop dance routines in the playground

When he's on the road, Howie misses his mum's home cooking

HOWIE LOVES A NIGHT OUT CLUBBING

He thinks being in love is great – and a bit frightening too

Even when he's not working, Howie likes to hang out with Kevin and AJ

HOWIE IS HALF SPANISH AND HALF ITALIAN

He thinks Brit singer Louise is super-sexy

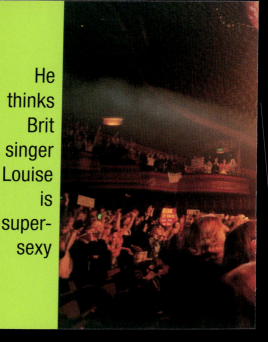

Howie's first stage performance was as a Munchkin in *The Wizard of Oz*!

According to the rest of the Backstreet Boys, Howie snores

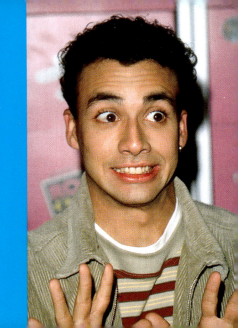

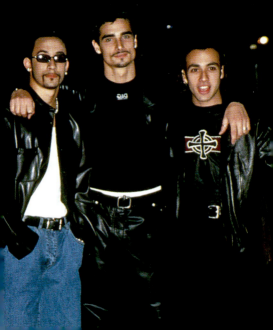

Howie says
he's the most
sensible
Backstreet Boy
when it comes
to money

HOWIE SAYS HE KNOWS ALL HIS BANDMATES' SECRETS!

When Howie was asked to sing the National Anthem at his school football match, he forgot the words!

Howie fancied being a show-biz lawyer if he wasn't a star

Howie sometimes argues with Brian and Nick — but says that the Backstreet Boys are just like brothers

HOWIE
WANTED TO BE
IN THE BAND
*NEW KIDS ON
THE BLOCK* AND
EVEN SENT
THEM A TAPE OF
HIM SINGING
THEIR SONGS

Howie is always the last on the tour bus, 'cos he's busy signing autographs

Howie says he is a workaholic

He's the

baby

of his

family

by ten

years